COMMUNITY SCHOOL

COMMUNITY HEALTH CLINIC

Welcome to My Maasai Life,
Robin Wiszowaty.

P.S. You can read my full story in my book,
My Maasai Life: From Suburbia to Savannah.

When I was younger, I was just like you.
I played with my friends after school.
I liked playing softball, but swimming
was my favorite sport!

After doing my homework after school, I would do my chores.
I would walk our dog Fluffy and vacuum the house.

I would even wash the dishes. (Don't tell my Mom, but I don't like doing chores!) All the while, I would daydream about Africa. I wanted to explore and see the animals! And when I was a little older than you, I got my wish.

I went on a trip…

On a sunny day, I say goodbye to my Mom and Dad at the airport and jump aboard an airplane. After a long trip over the ocean, I land in a new country in East Africa called **KENYA.**

I am excited to explore and meet the **MAASAi** (Ma-sigh) people.

I don't know what to expect...

I climb into a pickup truck in a market town. There are bright colors everywhere. People are busy buying food and clothes. As we drive, I spot some goats and chickens walking on the street.

Everyone speaks a language in Kenya called SWAHiLi (Swa-hee-lee). I don't understand anything!

We drive over some big hills into rural Kenya where the Maasai people live.

When we arrive in the Maasai community, I yell my first new words of Swahili to the driver:

"ASANTE!"

(Ah-sahn-tay; thank you.)

BOING

A tall, beautiful woman dressed in a blue and white dress comes forward. "My name is Mama. Here is our community. Come meet my family," she says.

Mama takes my hand and we explore.
We pass a school made of wood.
We pass a health clinic made of stone bricks.
And then we pass some short houses
made of mud and sticks.

They don't look like my house back home.

Mama turns toward one of the small huts and says:

Beside me two cows lick my hand. It sure is different from my home.

"This is where we keep our cows. They are important because they give us milk every day," says Mama.

"KARIBU!"

(Cah-ree-boo; welcome.)

We duck our heads into the small house made of mud, cow dung and sticks. "This is where we sleep," Mama says. It is dark inside, but there is a fire.

"And this is where we cook," Mama explains, pointing to the smoky fire.

Outside the mud house, Mama's family is smiling at me.
There is Grandma, Mama, Dad, three daughters and four sons. There are cows,
goats, sheep and chickens. What a big family! One of the young girls steps forward.

"KARIBU!" My name is Faith. Want to help me cook?"
"But I have never cooked over a fire," I say.
"Come, I'll show you."

Inside the home we sit on small benches. Faith balances a pot on top of three stones. She stokes the fire with a long stick.

Faith removes the pot and hands out eleven servings of her favorite dish called UGALi (oo-gall-ee) which she eats every day. Faith adds another log to the fire.

"SQUAWK!"

("Hello," in chicken speak)

But where does all the firewood come from, I ask.
"We go to the forest to collect it," she tells me. "Want to help?"
Sure, an adventure! I follow Faith down a winding path.

She shows me how to hack the dried branches. (The knife is so big and sharp).

SWOOOOOSH!

Faith ties the piles of wood so we can carry them on our backs. I can't believe how heavy it is! I struggle to follow Faith as she walks back down the path.

While I huff and puff carrying the firewood, Faith asks me a question.
"How far do you walk to collect your firewood?"
"We don't cook over a fire. We cook with electricity. We have a stove, an oven and a microwave to heat our food," I say.

"What is a mi-cro-wave?" Faith asks, trying to say the new word.
"It looks like a box. You press buttons to tell it how long to cook the food."

Faith looks confused.

We then hear something moving in the tall grass behind us. We stay silent.
We see a zebra! Then another zebra and another!
We count 11 big zebras and two babies.

When we get back, I show Mama my firewood. She smiles and asks if I want to fetch water.

My back hurts from the firewood, but I want to explore more.

Faith and I walk for 20 minutes under the hot sun until we see a flowing river. The water is brown. It looks like chocolate milk.
"It isn't very clean, but we don't have any other water," Faith explains.

Faith leans over and fills her barrel. She then straps it on her back. I try to copy her but I fall over. It is soooo heavy!

Faith laughs at me and balances the barrel on my back.

HA HA HA

THUMP!

"Faith, can we take a rest?" I ask.
We lean against the tree trunk of an **ACACiA** (ah-kay-shah) tree to relax.

"Robin, if you aren't used to carrying water, where do you get it from?" asks Faith.
"We have sinks with taps. You turn the tap and water comes out."
She shrugs her shoulders and laughs.

Faith points to the sun and says we should go home.

Just then we see a tall giraffe in the distance. It is followed by six more giraffes!

At home, we only see squirrels or cats or dogs. Sometimes a rabbit, but never a giraffe. Excited by our discovery, Faith and I skip home. But we are careful not to spill our water.

Mama is waiting for us with the cows.

She is very thankful for our help with the chores. We drink CHAI (chah-ee, tea) between chores.

"I know you must be tired," says Mama.

"ASANTE", I say, remembering some Swahili.

GLUG GLUG GLUG

While we drink our chai, Mama's children sing to the cows.
"My children always sing to the cows while they herd.
They can sing all day and all night!"

I begin to think about my home.
I want to tell Mom and Dad about
Mama, Faith, the giraffes
and the life they live here.

Some things are so similar to
home, and some are so different.

Before the sun hides its face, Faith takes me to see her new school.
It is small but it has bright blue paint and a few desks inside.

There is a chalkboard with some words on it.
I write my name on the chalkboard. Faith does the same.
To practice, I also write the SWAHiLi words I learned.

Children are playing soccer behind the school.
They call Faith and me over to join them.

We play until it gets dark outside. Then we go back home for bedtime.
I can't wait to tell Mom and Dad about my MAASAi LiFE!

When I get back from **KENYA,** I sit around the tree behind our house and tell Mom and Dad about my trip and what I learned.

After carrying water and cutting firewood, I tell my parents that we could be more aware of saving water and electricity by turning off taps and lights after we use them.

And this time, I promised them, I would be more than willing to help out with chores around the house!

GLOSSARY OF TERMS:

KENYA: A COUNTRY IN EAST AFRICA

SWAHILI: LANGUAGE USED IN PARTS OF EAST AFRICA

MAASAI: AN ETHNIC GROUP OF RURAL HERDERS IN KENYA

ASANTE: THANK YOU   **KARIBU:** WELCOME

UGALI: COMMON FOOD MADE OF CORN FLOUR AND WATER

ACACIA: A TREE COMMON IN AFRICA

CHAI: TEA

FREE THE CHILDREN
children helping children through education

ABOUT FREE THE CHILDREN:

Free The Children is the world's largest network of children helping children through education, with more than one million youth involved in its innovative education and development programs in 45 countries. Founded in 1995 by international child rights activist Craig Kielburger, Free The Children has a remarkable record of achievement, initiating development projects around the world and inspiring young people to develop as socially conscious global citizens. Today, through the voices and actions of youth, Free The Children has built more than 600 sustainable schools in developing countries around the world. Under the Adopt a Village model, Free The Children supports the communities by providing primary education, health care, alternative income projects and clean water to create sustainable communities.

Visit www.freethechildren.com to learn more.

me to we

ABOUT ME TO WE:

Me to We is a new kind of social enterprise for people who want to help change the world with their daily choices. Through our media, products and leadership experiences, we support Free The Children's work with youth creating global change. Every trip, organic and free-trade T-shirt, song, book, speech, thought, smile and choice adds up to a lifestyle that's part of the worldwide movement of *we*. Me to We offers choices that allow people to create ripples of positive change. What's more, Me to We is designed to help bring Free The Children's already low administrative costs to zero. Half of its annual profits are given to Free The Children with the other half reinvested to sustain the growth of the enterprise.

Visit www.metowe.com to find out more.

ME TO WE SPEAKERS

Bring me as a speaker to your school—and take away all you need to "be the change." The team at Me to We Speakers has traveled the world to discover the most inspirational people with remarkable stories and life experiences. From community activists to former child soldiers to social entrepreneurs, our roster of energetic, experienced speakers are leading the me to we movement: living and working in developing communities, helping businesses achieve social responsibility and inspiring auditoriums of youth and educators to action. Our stories and powerful messages inspire, motivate and educate. We leave audiences with a desire to take action and make a difference. We will make you laugh, cry and gain new perspective on what really matters. Be warned: our passion is contagious!

Visit www.metowe.com/speakers to learn more.

ME TO WE TRIPS

Come join me in Kenya on a Me to We Trip. If you want to really experience another culture and truly see the world, take a Me to We Trip. Seek out a volunteer travel experience as a family and see the beautiful Maasailand. Our staff live and work in the communities you'll visit, coordinating schoolbuilding and supporting development in participation with local communities. On a Me to We Trip, you'll learn leadership skills, experience new cultures and forge truly meaningful connections. Over 3,000 adventurous people of all ages have chosen to volunteer abroad with us. You'll do incredible things like building schools and assisting on clean water projects. You'll meet exuberant children excited at new possibilities for learning, and be immersed in local communities in ways never otherwise possible. And best of all, you'll have memories that last a lifetime.

Visit www.metowe.com/trips to learn more.

BUY A BOOK, GIVE A BOOK

The Buy a Book, Give a Book promise
ensures that for every Me to We book purchased,
a notebook will be given
to a child in a developing country.

ME TO WE BOOKS

My Maasai Life
Robin Wiszowaty

In her early 20s, Robin Wiszowaty left the ordinary world behind to join a traditional Maasai family. In the sweeping vistas and dusty footpaths of rural Kenya, she embraced a way of life unlike she'd ever known. With full-color photographs from her adventures, Robin's heart-wrenching story will inspire you to question your own definitions of home, happiness and family.

The World Needs Your Kid: Raising Children Who Care and Contribute
Craig Kielburger and Marc Kielburger and Shelley Page

This unique guide to parenting is centred on a simple but profound philosophy that will encourage children to become global citizens. Drawing on life lessons from such remarkable individuals as Jane Goodall, Mia Farrow and Archbishop Desmond Tutu, award-winning journalist Shelley Page and Marc and Craig Kielburger demonstrate how small actions make huge differences in the life of a child and can ultimately change the world.

Free the Children
Craig Kielburger

This is the story that launched a movement. Free the Children recounts twelve-year-old Craig Kielburger's remarkable odyssey across South Asia, meeting some of the world's most disadvantaged children, exploring slums and sweatshops, fighting to rescue children from the chains of inhumane conditions. Winner of the prestigious Christopher Award, Free the Children has been translated into eight languages and inspired young people around the world.

The Making of an Activist
Craig and Marc Kielburger with Lekha Singh

Warning: this book will change you. Full of vivid images and inspiring words, travelogues, poems and sparkling artwork, The Making of an Activist is more than just a scrapbook of Free The Children's remarkable evolution. It's a testament to living an engaged, active and compassionate life, painting an intimate portrait of powerful young activists. Explore the book. Catch the spark.

It Takes a Child
Craig Kielburger and Marisa Antonello; Illustrated by Turnstyle Imaging

It was an ordinary morning like any other. Twelve-year-old Craig Kielburger woke to his alarm clock and hurried downstairs to wolf down a bowl of cereal over the newspaper's comics before school. But what he discovered on the paper's front page would change his life—and eventually affect over a million young people worldwide. It Takes a Child is a fun, vibrant look back at Craig's adventures throughout South Asia, learning about global poverty and child labour. This incredible story truly demonstrates you're never too young to change the world.

Visit www.metowe.com/books to learn more.